A

The Open Group Publications available from Van Haren Publishing

The TOGAF Series:
TOGAF® Version 9.1
TOGAF® Version 9.1 – A Pocket Guide
TOGAF® 9 Foundation Study Guide, 2nd Edition
TOGAF® 9 Certified Study Guide, 2nd Edition

The Open Group Series:
Cloud Computing for Business – The Open Group Guide
ArchiMate® 2.0 Specification
ArchiMate® 2.0 – A Pocket Guide

The Open Group Security Series:
Open Information Security Management Maturity Model (O-ISM3)
Open Enterprise Security Architecture (O-ESA)
Risk Management – The Open Group Guide

All titles are available to purchase from:
www.opengroup.org
www.vanharen.net
and also many international and online distributors.

ArchiMate® 2.0

A POCKET GUIDE

Title:	ArchiMate® 2.0 – A Pocket Guide
Series:	The Open Group Series
A Publication of:	The Open Group
Author:	Andrew Josey et al
Publisher:	Van Haren Publishing, Zaltbommel, www.vanharen.net
ISBN Hardcopy: ISBN eBook: ISBN ePUB:	978 90 8753 696 1 978 90 8753 960 3 978 90 8753 970 2
Edition:	First edition, first impression, March 2012 First edition, second impression with minor corrections, March 2013
Layout and Cover Design:	CO2 Premedia, Amersfoort – NL
Print:	Wilco, Amersfoort – NL
Copyright:	© The Open Group 2012. All rights reserved

ArchiMate® 2.0
A Pocket Guide
Document Number: G121

Published by The Open Group, January 2012.

Comments relating to the material contained in this document may be submitted to:

The Open Group
Apex Plaza
Forbury Road
Reading
Berkshire, RG1 1AX
United Kingdom

or by electronic mail to: ogspecs@opengroup.org

For any further enquiries about Van Haren Publishing, please send an email to:
info@vanharen.net

Contents

Preface

This Document

This is the Pocket Guide to ArchiMate 2.0, an Open Group Standard. It is intended to help architects by providing a reference for the ArchiMate graphical modeling language and also assist managers in understanding the basics of ArchiMate. It is organized as follows:

- Chapter 1 provides a high-level introduction to ArchiMate and its relationship to enterprise architecture.
- Chapter 2 describes the construction of the ArchiMate language, including an introduction to the core concepts, relationships, layering, and the ArchiMate framework.
- Chapter 3 describes the Business Layer, which includes the modeling concepts relevant in the business domain.
- Chapter 4 describes the Application Layer, which includes modeling concepts relevant for software applications.
- Chapter 5 describes the Technology Layer, which includes modeling concepts relevant for system software applications and infrastructure.
- Chapter 6 describes the relationships that the ArchiMate language includes to model the links between elements, and also the relationships to model the cross-layer dependencies between the Business, Application, and Technology Layers.
- Chapter 7 describes the Motivation Extension, which adds motivational concepts such as goal, principle, and requirement to the language.
- Chapter 8 describes the Implementation and Migration Extension, which adds concepts to support the implementation and migration of enterprise architectures.
- Chapter 9 describes the ArchiMate framework for defining and classifying ArchiMate viewpoints, and provides a summary of the viewpoints included in the ArchiMate 2.0 Standard.

- Chapter 10 includes the ArchiSurance Case Study, a fictitious example developed to illustrate use of the ArchiMate modeling language in the context of the TOGAF framework.

The audience for this document is:

- Enterprise architects, business architects, IT architects, application architects, data architects, software architects, systems architects, solutions architects, infrastructure architects, process architects, domain architects, product managers, operational managers and senior managers seeking a first introduction to the ArchiMate modeling language.

After reading this document, the reader seeking further information should refer to the ArchiMate documentation[1] available online at www.opengroup.org/archimate.

Conventions Used in this Document

The following conventions are used throughout this document in order to help identify important information and avoid confusion over the intended meaning:

- Ellipsis (…)
  Indicates a continuation; such as an incomplete list of example items, or a continuation from preceding text.
- **Bold**
  Used to highlight specific terms.
- *Italics*
  Used for emphasis. May also refer to other external documents.

---

1 ArchiMate 2.0 (ISBN: 978 90 8753 692 3, C118); refer to www.opengroup.org/bookstore/catalog/c118.htm.

In addition to typographical conventions, the following convention is used to highlight segments of text:

 A Note box is used to highlight useful or interesting information.

About The Open Group

The Open Group is a global consortium that enables the achievement of business objectives through IT standards. With more than 400 member organizations, The Open Group has a diverse membership that spans all sectors of the IT community – customers, systems and solutions suppliers, tool vendors, integrators, and consultants, as well as academics and researchers – to:

• Capture, understand, and address current and emerging requirements, and establish policies and share best practices

• Facilitate interoperability, develop consensus, and evolve and integrate specifications and open source technologies

• Offer a comprehensive set of services to enhance the operational efficiency of consortia

• Operate the industry's premier certification service

Further information on The Open Group is available at www.opengroup.org.

Trademarks

About the Authors

Andrew Josey, The Open Group

Andrew Josey is Director of Standards within The Open Group. He is currently managing the standards process for The Open Group, and has recently led the standards development projects for ArchiMate 2.0 and TOGAF 9.1, IEEE Std 1003.1-2008 (POSIX), and the core specifications of the Single UNIX Specification, Version 4. He is a member of the IEEE, USENIX, UKUUG, and the Association of Enterprise Architects (AEA).

Steve Else, EA Principals

Steve is CEO and Chief Architect of EA Principals. Steve has successfully combined wearing many hats as an Enterprise Architect. He was a practitioner as Chief Enterprise Architect at the Office of Inspector General, Department of Health and Human Services (2008-2010); educator as Adjunct Professor Enterprise Architecture at the graduate level for four years and counting; consultant/contractor to Fortune 1000 companies for enterprise architecture deliverables; and training TOGAF globally – now in his sixth year. He is the Founder and Chair of the Association of Enterprise Architects Chapter in the Washington, DC area (AEA-DC).

Henry Franken, BiZZdesign

Henry Franken is the managing director of BiZZdesign, and is chair of The Open Group ArchiMate Forum. As chair of The Open Group ArchiMate Forum, Henry led the development of the ArchiMate 2.0 Standard. Henry is a speaker at many conferences and has co-authored several international publications and Open Group White Papers. Henry is co-founder of the BPM-Forum. At BiZZdesign, Henry is responsible for research and innovation.

Henk Jonkers, BiZZdesign

Henk Jonkers is a Senior Research Consultant at BiZZdesign. In this capacity, he is involved in the company's new developments in the area of enterprise architecture and enterprise engineering. He also participates in multi-party research projects, contributes to training courses, and performs consultancy assignments. Previously, he worked as a Member of Scientific Staff at Telematica Instituut (currently Novay), where he was involved in various applied research projects in the areas of business process modeling and analysis, enterprise architecture, service-oriented architecture, and model-driven development. Henk was one of the main developers of ArchiMate and an author of the ArchiMate 1.0 and 2.0 specifications, and is actively involved in the activities of The Open Group ArchiMate Forum.

Iver Band, Standard Insurance Company

Iver Band chairs The Open Group ArchiMate Forum Work Group on Insurance Industry Reference Models and is an enterprise architect at Standard Insurance Company. Earlier, he was a security architect and researcher at HP, where he led development of a patented method for network security management. Iver has been a CISSP since 2005.

Dick Quartel, BiZZdesign

Dick Quartel is a Senior Research Consultant at BiZZdesign. In this role he contributes to the development and improvement of BiZZdesign's products and services, is involved in research projects, supervises MSc students and interns, and performs consultancy assignments. In addition, he is an author of many scientific and professional publications, and an author of the ArchiMate 2.0 Standard. Previously, he worked as a Senior Researcher at Novay (formerly Telematica Instituut), where he acted as researcher and project manager and contributed to the definition and acquisition of research projects, and as an Assistant Professor at the University of Twente in the areas of distributed systems design, protocol design and implementation, and middleware systems.

Simon Parker, IBM UK Ltd.

Simon Parker is an Enterprise Architecture and Technology Strategy
Consultant within IBM Global Business Services. He has over 20 years'
experience across a range of Information Technology roles including
strategy, architecture, design, development, and support. Prior to joining
IBM, Simon worked in end-user organizations in the Energy Utility and
Central Government sectors. He has a Master of Science in Managing
IT and is TOGAF certified and trained. Simon has practical rather than
purely theoretical experience of using EA methods and tools, creating EA
artifacts, providing assessments, and mentoring others – all of which means
he is well aware of the value and pitfalls of establishing and operating an
EA capability.

Paul Homan, IBM UK Ltd.

Paul Homan is a Technology Strategy Consultant within IBM's Global
Business Services. He is a Certified Master IT Architect, specializing in
enterprise architecture, with over 20 years' experience in IT. Paul joined
IBM from end-user environments, having worked as Chief Architect in
both the UK Post Office and Royal Mail. He has not only established
enterprise architecture practices, but has also lived with the results!
Since joining IBM, Paul has dedicated his time to both advising clients
on architecture capability as well as actively leading architecture efforts
on large client programs. Paul has also been a leader in building IBM's
capability around enterprise architecture and TOGAF.

Acknowledgements

The Open Group gratefully acknowledges the following:

- Past and present members of The Open Group ArchiMate Forum for developing the ArchiMate Standard.
- BiZZdesign BV and Novay, and its predecessors Telematica Institut and Telematica Research Center, for the previous work on the ArchiSurance Case Study.
- The following reviewers of this document:
  - Bill Estrem
  - Rafal Jablonka
  - Judith Jones
  - Russel Jones
  - Philip King
  - Michael Novak
  - Doug Rinker
  - Andrzej Sobczak
  - Serge Thorn
  - Fawn Wu

Chapter 1
Introduction

This chapter provides an introduction to ArchiMate, an Open Group Standard.

Topics addressed in this chapter include:

- An introduction to ArchiMate
- A brief overview of ArchiMate
- ArchiMate and its relationship to enterprise architecture and TOGAF

1.1 Introduction to ArchiMate

ArchiMate, an Open Group Standard, is an open and independent modeling language for enterprise architecture that is supported by different tool vendors and consulting firms. ArchiMate provides a notation to enable enterprise architects to describe, analyze, and visualize the relationships among business domains in an unambiguous way.

Just as an architectural drawing in classical building architecture describes the various aspects of the construction and use of a building, ArchiMate offers a common language for describing the construction and operation of business processes, organizational structures, information flows, IT systems, and technical infrastructure. This insight helps stakeholders to design, assess, and communicate the consequences of decisions and changes within and between these business domains.

ArchiMate was created in the period 2002-2004 in the Netherlands by a project team from the Telematica Instituut in co-operation with several partners from government, industry, and academia, including Ordina, Radboud Universiteit Nijmegen, the Leiden Institute for Advanced Computer Science (LIACS), and the Centrum Wiskunde & Informatica (CWI). The development included tests in organizations such as ABN

AMRO, the Dutch Tax and Customs Administration, and the Stichting
Pensioenfonds ABP. In 2008, the ownership and stewardship of ArchiMate
was transferred from the ArchiMate Foundation to The Open Group. It is
now managed by The Open Group ArchiMate Forum. In February 2009,
The Open Group published ArchiMate 1.0 as an Open Group Standard.

The ArchiMate 2.0 Specification
This document provides an introduction to the ArchiMate 2.0 specification,
referred to simply as "ArchiMate" within the main text of this document.
The ArchiMate 2.0 specification was approved as an Open Group Standard
in October 2011 and published in January 2012.

1.2 ArchiMate Specification Overview

The ArchiMate 2.0 specification is The Open Group standard for the
ArchiMate Architecture Modeling Language. The standard contains the
formal definition of ArchiMate as a visual design language, together with
concepts for specifying inter-related architectures, and specific viewpoints
for typical stakeholders. The standard also includes a chapter addressing
considerations regarding language extensions.

The contents of the standard include the following:

- The overall modeling framework that ArchiMate uses
- The structure of the modeling language
- A detailed breakdown of the constituent elements of the modeling
  framework covering the three layers (Business/Application/Technology),
  cross-layer dependencies and alignment, and relationships within the
  framework
- Architectural viewpoints including a set of standard viewpoints
- Optional extensions to the framework
- Commentary around future direction of the specification
- Notation overviews and summaries

ArchiMate 2.0 is an evolution of ArchiMate 1.0 in that it includes
corrections, improvements, and clarifications to the original published

specification as well as the addition of two optional extensions (Motivation and Implementation and Migration).

The standard is complemented by additional documents including the ArchiSurance Case Study, an abridged version of which is included in this Pocket Guide, and the ArchiMate certification program, which covers People Certification, Training Course Accreditation, and Tools Certification.

1.3 ArchiMate and Enterprise Architecture

The role of the ArchiMate standard is to provide a graphical language for the representation of enterprise architectures over time (i.e., including transformation and migration planning), as well as their motivation and rationale. The ArchiMate modeling language provides a uniform representation for diagrams that describe enterprise architectures, and offers an integrated approach to describe and visualize the different architecture domains together with their underlying relations and dependencies.

The design of the ArchiMate language started from a set of relatively generic concepts (objects and relations), which have been specialized for application at the different architectural layers for an enterprise architecture. The most important design restriction on ArchiMate is that it has been explicitly designed to be as compact as possible, yet still usable for most enterprise architecture modeling tasks. In the interest of simplicity of learning and use, ArchiMate has been limited to the concepts that suffice for modeling the proverbial 80% of practical cases.

1.3.1 ArchiMate Core, Extensions, and the TOGAF ADM

ArchiMate 2.0 consists of the ArchiMate Core (the core language), that focuses on the description of the four architecture domains defined by the TOGAF standard (business, data, application, and technology architectures, as well as their inter-relationships), and extensions to model the motivations for the architecture, and its implementation and migration planning. Figure 1 shows how the ArchiMate Core, the Motivation Extension, and the Implementation and Migration Extension relate to the phases of the TOGAF ADM.

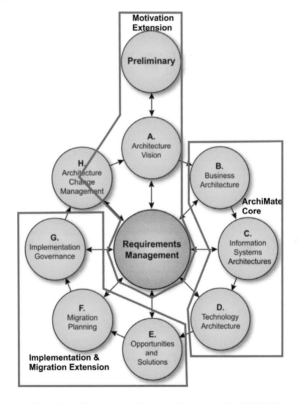

Figure 1: The Relationship between ArchiMate Core, Extensions, and the TOGAF ADM

The Motivation Extension concepts in ArchiMate support the Requirements Management, Preliminary Phase, and Architecture Vision phases of the TOGAF ADM, which establish the high-level business goals, architecture principles, and initial business requirements. It is also relevant to the Architecture Change Management phase of the TOGAF ADM, since the phase deals with changing requirements.

The Implementation and Migration Extension of ArchiMate adds concepts to support the implementation and migration of architectures through the Opportunities and Solutions, Migration Planning, and Implementation Governance phases of the TOGAF ADM.

Chapter 2
Language Structure

This chapter describes the construction of the ArchiMate language. Topics addressed in this chapter include:

- Core concepts of the ArchiMate language
- Collaboration and interaction
- Relationships
- Layering
- The ArchiMate framework

2.1 Core Concepts of the ArchiMate Language

The core language consists of three types of elements, as shown in Figure 2:

- Active structure elements
- Behavior elements
- Passive structure elements (objects)

These three aspects – active structure, behavior, and passive structure – have been inspired by natural language, where a sentence has a subject (active structure), a verb (behavior), and an object (passive structure).

In addition to the three elements, ArchiMate makes a distinction between an external view and an internal view of a system by defining *service* and *interface*.

Conventions for the Use of Colors

In the metamodel diagrams within the ArchiMate Standard and this document, colors are used to distinguish concepts belonging to the different aspects of the ArchiMate framework (see Figure 4): green is used for passive structure, yellow for behavior, and blue for active structure. In ArchiMate models, there are no formal semantics assigned to colors. However, they can be used freely to stress certain aspects in models. For instance, in the example models presented in the standard, colors are often used to distinguish between the layers of the ArchiMate framework: yellow for the Business Layer, blue for the Application Layer, and green for the Technology Layer.

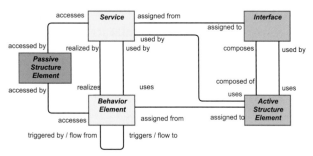

Figure 2: Generic Metamodel: The Core Concepts of ArchiMate

2.1.1 Active Structure Element

An **active structure element** is defined as an entity that is capable of performing behavior. Examples are the business actors, application components, and devices that display actual behavior; i.e., the subjects of activity as shown in the right side of Figure 2.

2.1.2 Behavior Element

A **behavior element** is defined as a unit of activity performed by one or more **active structure elements**. These show who or what performs the behavior for an **active structure element** construct as shown in the center of Figure 2.

2.1.3 Passive Structure Element

A **passive structure element** is defined as an object on which behavior is performed as shown in the left side of Figure 2. These are usually information or data objects, and may also represent physical objects.

2.1.4 Service

A **service** is defined as a unit of functionality that a system exposes to its environment which provides a certain value. The **service** is the externally visible behavior of the providing system. For users of the service only the exposed functionality and value (which can be monetary or otherwise) are relevant. **Services** are accessible through **interfaces**.

2.1.5 Interface

An **interface** is defined as a point of access where one or more services are made available to the environment. **Interfaces** constitute the external view on **active structure elements**, and provide access to **services**.

2.2 Collaboration and Interaction

Going one level deeper in the structure of the language, there is a distinction between behavior that is performed by a single structure element (e.g., actor, role component, etc.), or collective behavior (interaction) that is performed by a collaboration of multiple structure elements.

2.2.1 Collaboration

A **collaboration** is defined as a (temporary) grouping (or aggregation) of two or more structure elements, working together to perform some collective behavior.

2.2.2 Interaction

This collective behavior can be modeled as an **interaction**. An interaction
is defined as a unit of behavior performed by a collaboration of two or
more structure elements.

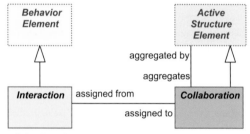

Figure 3: Collaboration and Interaction

2.3 Relationships

Next to the core concepts outlined above, ArchiMate contains a core set
of relationships. Several of these relationships have been adopted from
corresponding relationship concepts that occur in existing standards. For
example, relationships such as composition, aggregation, association, and
specialization are taken from UML 2.0, while triggering is used in many
business process modeling languages. Further information on relationships
is described in Chapter 6.

2.4 Layering

The ArchiMate language defines three layers (depicted with different colors
in the examples in the next chapters), based on specializations of the core
concepts described in Section 2.1 and 2.2.

1. The **Business Layer** offers products and services to external customers, which are realized in the organization by business processes performed by business actors. The Business Layer is described in Chapter 3.
2. The **Application Layer** supports the Business Layer with application services which are realized by (software) applications. The Application Layer is described in Chapter 4.
3. The **Technology Layer** offers infrastructure services (e.g., processing, storage, and communication services) needed to support applications, realized by computer and communication hardware and system software. The Technology Layer is described in Chapter 5.

The general structure of models within the different layers is similar. The same types of concepts and relationships are used, although their exact nature and granularity differ.

The most important relationship between layers is formed by "used by" relationships, which show how the higher layers make use of the services of lower layers. A second type of link is formed by realization relationships: elements in lower layers may realize comparable elements in higher layers. For example, a "data object" (Application Layer) may realize a "business object" (Business Layer); or an "artifact" (Technology Layer) may realize either a "data object" or an "application component" (Application Layer).

2.5 The ArchiMate Framework
The aspects and layers identified in the previous sections can be organized as a framework of nine "cells", as illustrated in Figure 4.

Besides the elements shown in Figure 4 (passive structure, behavior, and active structure), which are mainly operational in nature, an enterprise architect touches upon numerous other aspects in the course of his/her

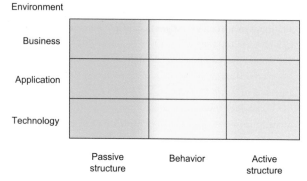

Figure 4: ArchiMate Framework

work that are not explicitly covered by the ArchiMate framework, some of which may cross several (or all) conceptual domains; for example:

- Goals, principles, and requirements
- Risk and security
- Governance
- Policies and business rules
- Costs
- Performance
- Timing
- Planning and evolution

Not all of these aspects can be completely covered using the standard language extension mechanisms. In order to facilitate the work of tool vendors and methodology experts in providing support for additional aspects within the overall ArchiMate language, specific extensions can be added. Modular extensions can add new language concepts, relationships, or attributes, while complying to ArchiMate's core design goal: to be as compact as possible.

ArchiMate 2.0 includes two such extensions: the **Motivation Extension** and the **Implementation and Migration Extension** (see Section 1.3.1, Chapter 7, and Chapter 8).

Chapter 3
Business Layer

The Business Layer includes a number of additional concepts beyond
the generic metamodel introduced in Figure 2, which are relevant in the
business domain. This includes a product and an associated contract, the
meaning of business objects, and the value of products of business services.
As with all the architecture layers (Business, Application, and Technology),
structure, behavior, and information concepts are central. These are
summarized in the following sections.

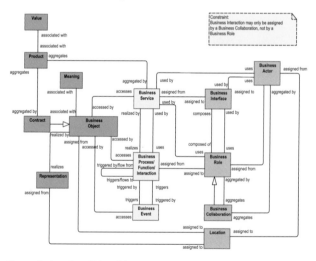

Figure 5: Business Layer Metamodel

3.1 Structural Concepts

The structure aspect at the Business Layer refers to the static structure of an organization, in terms of the entities that make up the organization and their relationships.

Two types of entities are distinguished:
- The **active entities** that are the subjects (e.g., business actors or business roles) that perform behavior such as business processes or functions (capabilities). Business actors may be individual persons (e.g., customers or employees), or groups of people (organization units), and resources that have a permanent (or at least long-term) status within the organizations. Typical examples of the latter are a department and a business unit.
- The **passive entities** are business objects that are manipulated by behavior such as business processes or functions. The passive entities represent the important concepts in which the business thinks about a domain.

Table 1: Business Layer – Structural Concepts

Concept	Description	Notation
Business actor	An organizational entity that is capable of performing behavior. A business actor performs the behavior assigned to (one or more) business roles. The name of a business actor should be a noun.	Business actor
Business role	The responsibility for performing specific behavior, to which an actor can be assigned. A business role may be assigned to one or more business processes or business functions. The name of a business role should be a noun.	Business role

Concept	Description	Notation
Business collaboration	An aggregate of two or more business roles that work together to perform collective behavior. Business interactions are used to describe the internal behavior that takes place within business collaboration. The name of a business collaboration should be a noun. It is also common to leave a business collaboration unnamed.	Business collaboration
Business interface	A point of access where a business service is made available to the environment. A business interface exposes the functionality of a business service to other business roles, or expects functionality from other business services. The name of a business interface should be a noun.	Business interface
Location	A conceptual point or extent in space. The location concept is used to model the distribution of structural elements such as business actors, application components, and devices.	Location
Business object	A passive element that has relevance from a business perspective. Business objects represent the important informational or conceptual elements in which the business thinks about a domain. Business objects are passive in the sense that they do not trigger or perform processes. The name of a business object should be a noun.	Business object

3.2 Behavioral Concepts

Based on service-orientation, a crucial design decision for the behavioral part of the ArchiMate metamodel is the distinction between "external" and "internal" behavior of an organization.

The externally visible behavior is modeled by the concept **business service**. A distinction can be made between "external" business services, offered to external customers, and "internal" business services, offering supporting functionality to processes or functions within the organization.

Several types of internal behavior elements that can realize a service are distinguished: a **process view** and a **function view** on behavior; two concepts associated with these views, **business process** and **business function**, are defined. A **business interaction** is a unit of behavior similar to a business process or function but which is performed in a collaboration of two or more roles within the organization.

A **business event** is something that happens (externally) and may influence business processes, functions, or interactions.

Table 2: Business Layer – Behavioral Concepts

Concept	Description	Notation
Business process	A behavior element that groups behavior based on an ordering of activities. It is intended to produce a defined set of products or business services. In an ArchiMate model, the existence of business processes is depicted. It does not, however, list the flow of activities in detail. The name of a business process should be a verb in the simple present tense; for example, "handle claim".	Business process

Concept	Description	Notation
Business function	A behavior element that groups behavior based on a chosen set of criteria (typically required business resources and/or competences). A business function may be triggered by, or trigger, any other business behavior element. The name of a business function should be a verb ending with "-ing" (for example, "claims processing"), or a noun ending in "-ion" or "-ment" (for example, "administration").	Business function
Business interaction	A behavior element that describes the behavior of a business collaboration. The roles in the collaboration share the responsibility for performing the interaction. The name of a business interaction should be a verb in the simple present tense.	Business interaction
Business event	Something that happens (internally or externally) and influences behavior. A business event may trigger or be triggered (raised) by a business process, business function, or business interaction. The name of a business event should be a verb in the perfect tense; for example, "claim received".	Business event

Concept	Description	Notation
Business service	A service that fulfills a business need for a customer (internal or external to the organization). A business service exposes the functionality of business roles or collaborations to their environment. The name of a business service should be a verb ending with "-ing"; for example, "transaction processing". Alternately, a name containing the word "service" should be used.	Business service

3.3 Informational Concepts

In contrast to the structural and behavioral concepts, which are mainly concerned with the operational perspective of an enterprise, the informational concepts focus on the "intentional" perspective. These are passive entities. They provide a way to link the operational side of an organization to its business goals and the products that it offers to its customers. The ArchiMate standard also classifies the product concept itself, together with the related contract concept, as informational concepts.

Table 3: Business Layer – Informational Concepts

Concept	Description	Notation
Representation	A perceptible form of the information carried by a business object; for example, messages or documents. The name of a representation should be a noun.	Representation

Concept	Description	Notation
Meaning	The knowledge or expertise present in a business object or its representation, given a particular context. It is a description that expresses the intent of a representation. The name of a meaning should be a noun or noun phrase.	Meaning
Value	The relative worth, utility, or importance of a business service or product. The name of a value should be expressed as an action or state that can be performed or reached as a result of the corresponding service or product being available.	Value
Product	A coherent collection of services, accompanied by a contract/set of agreements, which is offered as a whole to (internal or external) customers. This definition describes financial, services-based, or information products that are common in information-intensive organizations, rather than physical products. The name of a product should be the name which is used in communication with customers, or a generic noun such as "travel insurance".	Product
Contract	A formal or informal specification of agreement that specifies the rights and obligations associated with a product. The name of a contract should be a noun.	Contract

3.4 Example

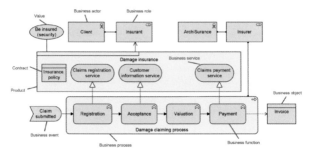

Figure 6: Example of a Business Layer Model

In this example, Client and ArchiSurance are **business actors**, the active entities that perform behavior such as business processes or functions. A **business role** is assigned to each actor. Client has the role of Insurant and makes use of the Damage insurance product. ArchiSurance has the role as an Insurer and is responsible for the Damage claiming **business process**, which is expressed by the assignment relation between the business process and the role. The Damage claiming process consists of four **business functions**.

In the example a distinction is made between "external" and "internal" behavior of ArchiSurance. The external visible behavior is modeled as **business services** that are realized by the internal **business functions** within the Damage claiming process. These business services, together with a **contract**, are grouped into a **product**. The **value** of the product in this example is to be "insured" or "security".

Chapter 4
Application Layer

The Application Layer describes software applications.

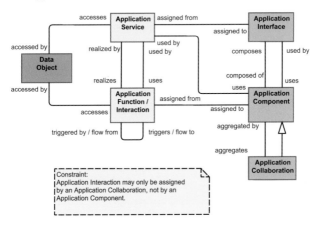

Figure 7: Application Layer Metamodel

4.1 Structural Concepts

The main structural concept for the Application Layer is the **application
component**. This concept is used to model any structural entity in the
Application Layer. It can describe (re-usable) software components that
can be part of one or more applications, and also complete software
applications, sub-applications, or information systems.

The concept of **application collaboration** is introduced here as the inter-
relationships of components are important in an application architecture.

It is defined as a collection of application components which perform application interactions.

An **application interface** is the (logical) channel through which the services of a component can be accessed. The application interface concept can be used to model both **application-to-application** interfaces, which offer internal application services, and **application-to business** interfaces (and/or **user interfaces**), which offer external application services.

Also at the Application Layer, the passive counterpart of the component is introduced, called a **data object**. A data object is a representation of a business object, as a counterpart of the representation concept in the Business Layer.

Table 4: Application Layer – Structural Concepts

Concept	Definition	Notation
Application component	A modular, deployable, and replaceable part of a software system that encapsulates its behavior and data and exposes these through a set of interfaces. An application component is a self-contained unit of functionality. The name of an application component should be a noun.	Application component
Application collaboration	An aggregate of two or more application components that work together to perform collective behavior. An application collaboration typically models a logical or temporary collaboration of application components. The name of an application collaboration should be a noun.	Application collaboration

Concept	Definition	Notation
Application interface	A point of access where an application service is made available to a user or another application component. An application interface specifies how the functionality of a component can be accessed by other components, or which functionality the component requires from its environment. The name of an application interface should be a noun.	Application interface
Data object	A passive element suitable for automated processing. It should be a self-contained piece of information with a clear meaning to the business, not just to the Application Level; for example, a customer record, a client database, or an insurance claim. The name of a data object should be a noun.	Data object

4.2 Behavioral Concepts

Behavior at the Application Layer is described in a similar way to Business Layer behavior. A distinction is made between the external behavior of application components in terms of **application services**, and the internal behavior of these components; i.e., **application functions** that realize these services.

An **application service** is an externally visible unit of functionality, provided by one or more components, exposed through well-defined interfaces, and meaningful to the environment. The functionality that an interactive computer program provides through a user interface is also modeled using an application service, exposed by an application-to-business interface representing the user interface. Internal application services are exposed through an application-to-application interface.

An **application function** describes the internal behavior of a component needed to realize one or more application services.

An **application interaction** is the behavior of a collaboration of two or more application components. An application interaction is external behavior from the perspective of each of the participating components, but the behavior is internal to the collaboration as a whole.

Table 5: Application Layer – Behavioral Concepts

Concept	Description	Notation
Application function	A behavior element that groups automated behavior that can be performed by an application component. An application function describes the internal behavior of an application component. The name of an application function should be a verb ending with "-ing"; for example, "accounting".	Application function
Application interaction	A behavior element that describes the behavior of an application collaboration. An application interaction describes the collective behavior that is performed by the components that participate in an application collaboration. The name of an application interaction should be a verb.	Application interaction

Concept	Description	Notation
Application service	A service that exposes automated behavior. An application service should be meaningful from the point of view of the environment; it should provide a unit of functionality that is in itself useful to its users. The name of an application service should be a verb ending with "-ing"; for example, "transaction processing". Alternately, a name containing the word "service" should be used.	Application service

4.3 Example

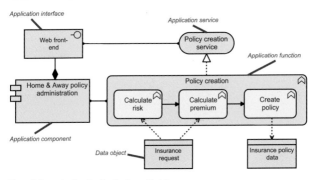

Figure 8: Example of an Application Layer Model

In this example, both **structural** and **behavioral** concepts of the Application Layer are illustrated. "Web front end" is the **application interface** that provides access to the **application service** called "Policy creation service". It is a composite part of the Home & Away policy administration **application component** (i.e., the application component exposes the application interface).

The "Policy creation" **application function** realizes the "Policy creation" **application service**. It is comprised of three lower level application functions – calculate risk, calculate premium, and create policy. These three application functions are linked by triggering dynamic relationships. The **data object** called "Insurance request" has an access structural relationship indicating that it is read by the "Calculate risk" and "Calculate premium" application functions, whilst the other data object shown, "Insurance policy data" is created by the "Create policy" application function.

Chapter 5
Technology Layer

The Technology Layer describes system software applications and
infrastructure. Whenever applicable, the ArchiMate language has drawn
analogies with the Business and Application Layers.

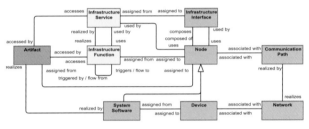

Figure 9: Technology Layer Metamodel

5.1 Structural Concepts

The main structural concept for the Technology Layer is the **node**. This
concept is used to model structural entities in this layer. An **infrastructure
interface** is the (logical) location where the infrastructure services offered
by a node can be accessed by other nodes or by application components
from the Application Layer.

The inter-relationships of components in the Technology Layer are mainly
formed by the communication infrastructure. The **communication
path** models the relation between two or more nodes, through which
these nodes can exchange information. The physical realization of
a communication path is modeled with a **network**; i.e., a physical
communication medium between two or more devices (or other networks).

Table 6: Technology Layer – Structural Concepts

Concept	Definition	Notation
Node	A computational resource upon which artifacts may be stored or deployed for execution. A node is often a combination of a hardware device and system software, thus providing a complete execution environment. The name of a node should be a noun. A node can consist of sub-nodes.	Node
Device	A hardware resource upon which artifacts may be stored or deployed for execution. A device is a specialization of a node that represents a physical resource with processing capability. It is typically used to model hardware systems such as mainframes, PCs, or routers. The name of a device should be a noun referring to the type of hardware.	Device
Network	A communication medium between two or more devices. A network represents the physical communication infrastructure. This may comprise one or more fixed or wireless network links. A network can consist of sub-networks.	Network

Concept	Definition	Notation
Communication path	A link between two or more nodes, through which these nodes can exchange data. A communication path is used to model the logical communication relations between nodes. It is realized by one or more networks, which represent the physical communication links.	
Infrastructure interface	A point of access where infrastructure services offered by a node can be accessed by other nodes and application components. An infrastructure interface specifies how the infrastructure services of a node can be accessed by other nodes, or which functionality the node requires from its environment. The name of an infrastructure interface should be a noun.	
System software	A software environment for specific types of components and objects that are deployed on it in the form of artifacts. System software is a specialization of a node that is used to model the software environment in which artifacts run. The name of system software should be a noun referring to the type of execution environment.	

5.2 Behavioral Concepts

Behavior elements in the Technology Layer are similar to the behavior elements in the other two layers. A distinction is made between the external behavior of nodes in terms of **infrastructure services**, and the internal behavior of these nodes; i.e., **infrastructure functions** that realize these services.

Table 7: Technology Layer – Behavioral Concepts

Concept	Description	Notation
Infrastructure function	A behavior element that groups infrastructural behavior that can be performed by a node. An infrastructure function describes the internal behavior of a node. The name of an infrastructure function should be a verb ending with "-ing".	Infrastructure function
Infrastructure service	An externally visible unit of functionality, provided by one or more nodes, exposed through well-defined interfaces, and meaningful to the environment. It should provide a unit of functionality that is in itself useful to its users, such as application components and nodes. The name of an infrastructure service should be a verb ending with "-ing"; for example, "messaging". Alternately, a name containing the word "service" should be used.	Infrastructure service

5.3 Informational Concepts

An **artifact** is the representation, for example, of a file, a data object, or an application component, and can be deployed on a node.

Table 8: Technology Layer – Informational Concepts

Concept	Description	Notation
Artifact	A physical piece of data that is used or produced in a software development process, or by deployment and operation of a system. It is typically used to model (software) products such as source files, executables, scripts, database tables, messages, documents, specifications, and model files. The name of an artifact should be the name of the data it represents.	Artifact

5.4 Example

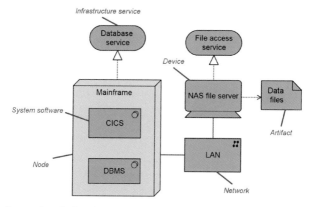

Figure 10: Example of a Technology Layer Model

In this example, **structural**, **behavioral**, and **informational** concepts
of the Technology Layer are illustrated. The structural technology
node "Mainframe" is shown to contain two **system software** elements
– CICS and DBMS. The "Mainframe" node is used in the delivery of
the **infrastructure service** "Database service", which is indicated by a
realization relationship.

The "Mainframe" node is linked to the "NAS file server" **device** via a
network, in this case a "LAN". The "NAS file server" facilitates the use of
information **artifacts** – "Data files". A second infrastructure service called
"File access service" is realized by the "NAS file server".

Chapter 6
Relationships and Cross-Layer Dependencies

This chapter describes the relationships that the ArchiMate language includes to model the links between objects, concepts, and elements. It also describes the relationships to model the cross-layer dependencies between the Business, Application, and Technology Layers.

6.1 Relationships

Relationships can be classified as either:

- **Structural**, which model the structural coherence of concepts of the same or different types
- **Dynamic**, which are used to model (temporal) dependencies between behavioral concepts
- **Other**, which do not fall into one of the two above categories

The following sections summarize the different relationships.

6.1.1 Structural Relationships

Table 9: Structural Relationships

Structural Relationships		Notation
Association	Association models a relationship between objects that is not covered by another, more specific relationship. It is used, as in UML, to model relationships between business objects or data objects that are not modeled by the standard relationships aggregation, composition, or specialization. In addition to this, it is used to link the informational concepts with the other concepts: a business object with a representation, a representation with a meaning, and a business service with a purpose.	——————

Structural Relationships		Notation
Access	The access relationship models the access of behavioral concepts to business or data objects. It is used to indicate that a process, function, interaction, service, or event "does something" with a (business or data) object. The relationship can also be used to indicate that the object is just associated with the behavior. The arrow head, if present, indicates the direction of the flow of information.	·········> ▪▪▪▪▪▪▪▪
Used by	The used by relationship models the use of services by processes, functions, or interactions and the access to interfaces by roles, components, or collaborations. It is used to describe the services that a role or component offers that are used by entities in the environment. The used by relationship is applied for both the behavior aspect and the structure aspect.	⟶
Realization	The realization relationship links a logical entity with a more concrete entity that realizes it. It indicates how logical entities ("what"), such as services, are realized by means of more concrete entities ("how"). It is used in an operational sense (e.g., a process/function realizes a service), and also in a design/implementation context (e.g., a data object may realize a business object, or an artifact may realize an application component).	·······▷
Assignment	The assignment relationship links units of behavior with active elements (e.g., roles, components) that perform them, or roles with actors that fulfill them. It can relate a business role with a business process or function, an application component with an application function, a business collaboration with a business interaction, an application collaboration with an application interaction, a business interface with a business service, an application interface with an application service, or a business actor with a business role.	●━━━●

Structural Relationships		Notation
Aggregation	The aggregation relationship indicates that an object groups a number of other objects. It is based on the aggregation relationship in UML class diagrams. In contrast to the composition relationship, an object can be part of more than one aggregation. In addition to aggregation relationships that are explicitly defined in the metamodel figures in this document, aggregation is always possible between two instances of the same concept.	◇————
Composition	The composition relationship indicates that an object is composed of one or more other objects. It is based on the composition relationship in UML class diagrams. In contrast to the aggregation relationship, an object can be part of only one composition. In addition to composition relationships that are explicitly defined in the metamodel figures in this document, composition is always possible between two instances of the same concept.	◆————

6.1.2 Dynamic Relationships

Table 10: Dynamic Relationships

Dynamic Relationships		Notation
Flow	The flow relationship describes the exchange or transfer of, for example, information or value between processes, function, interactions, and events. A flow relationship does not imply a causal or temporal relationship.	▪ ▪ ▪ ▶

Dynamic Relationships		Notation
Triggering	The triggering relationship describes the temporal or causal relationships between processes, functions, interactions, and events. No distinction is made between an active triggering relationship and a passive causal relationship.	⟶

6.1.3 Other Relationships

Table 11: Other Relationships

Other Relationships		Notation
Grouping	The grouping relationship indicates that objects, of the same type or different types, belong together based on some common characteristic. Unlike the other language concepts, grouping has no formal semantics. It is only used to show graphically that model elements have something in common. Model elements may belong to multiple (overlapping) groups.	
Junction	A junction is used to connect relationships of the same type. It is used in a number of situations to connect dynamic (triggering or flow) relationships of the same type; e.g., to indicate splits or joins.	●
Specialization	The specialization relationship indicates that an object is a specialization of another object.	⟶▷

6.1.4 Example

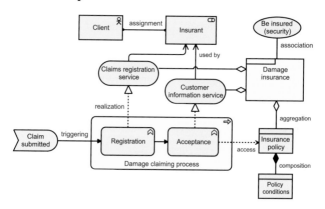

Figure 11: Example Model illustrating Relationships

Derived Relationships

In addition to the structural relationships described in the previous sections, ArchiMate includes an abstraction rule that makes it possible to determine indirect relationships between model elements. These are known as derived relationships. They can be useful for, amongst other things, impact analysis. Readers are referred to the ArchiMate Standard, Chapter 7 for more information.

6.2 Cross-Layer Dependencies

This section describes the relationships to model the cross-layer dependencies between business, applications, and technology.

6.2.1 Business-Application Alignment

Figure 12 shows the relationships between the Business Layer, the
Application Layer, and the Technology Layer concepts. There are three
main types of relationships between these layers:

1. **Used by** relationships, between application service and the different
   types of business behavior elements, and between application interface
   and business role.

2. A **realization** relationship from a data object to a business object,
   to indicate that the data object is a digital representation of the
   corresponding business object.

3. **Assignment** relationships, between application component and business
   process, function, or interaction, and between application interface and
   business service, to indicate that, for example, business processes or
   business services are completely automated.

In addition, an **aggregation** relationship between a product and an
application or infrastructure service may be used to indicate that the
application or infrastructure service can be offered directly to a customer
as part of the product. Also, a **location** may be assigned to all active and
passive structural elements (and, indirectly, behavior elements) in the
Application and Technology Layers.

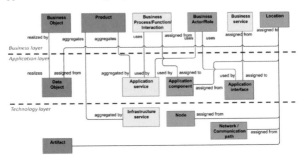

Figure 12: Relationships between Business Layer and Lower-Layer Concepts

6.2.2 Application-Technology Alignment

Figure 13 shows the relationships between Application Layer and Technology Layer concepts. There are two types of relationships between these layers:

1. **Used by** relationships, between infrastructure service and the different types of application behavior elements, and between infrastructure interface and application component. These relationships represent the behavioral and structural aspects of the use of technical infrastructure by applications.

2. A **realization** relationship from artifact to data object, to indicate that the data object is realized by, for example, a physical data file, and from artifact to application component, to indicate that a physical data file is an executable that realizes an application or part of an application.

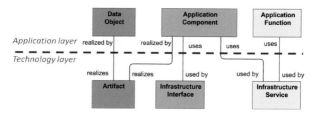

Figure 13: Relationships between Application Layer and Technology Layer Concepts

Chapter 7
The Motivation Extension

The Motivation Extension includes the motivational concepts such as **goal**, **principle**, and **requirement**. It addresses the way the enterprise architecture is aligned to its context, as described by motivational elements.

In addition, the Motivation Extension recognizes the concepts of **stakeholders**, **drivers**, and **assessments**. Stakeholders represent (groups of) persons or organizations that influence, guide, or constrain the enterprise. Drivers represent internal or external factors which influence the plans and aims of an enterprise. An understanding of strengths, weaknesses, opportunities, and threats in relation to these drivers will help the formation of plans and aims to appropriately address these issues.

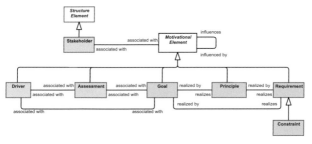

Figure 14: Motivation Extension Metamodel

The main reason to introduce this extension in ArchiMate is to support Requirements Management, the Preliminary Phase, and Phase A (Architecture Vision) of the TOGAF ADM.

7.1 Motivation Extension Concepts

Motivational concepts are used to model the motivations, or reasons, that underlie the design or change of the enterprise architecture. These motivations influence, guide, and constrain the design.

Table 12: Motivational Concepts

Concept	Definition	Notation
Stakeholder	The role of an individual, team, or organization (or classes thereof) that represents their interests in, or concerns relative to, the outcome of the architecture. In order to direct efforts to these interests and concerns, stakeholders change, set, and emphasize goals. The name of a stakeholder should be a noun.	Stakeholder
Driver	Something that creates, motivates, and fuels the change in an organization. Drivers may be internal, in which case they are associated with a stakeholder. Drivers may also be external; for example, changing legislation. The name of a driver should be a noun.	Driver
Assessment	The outcome of an analysis activity for a driver or set of related drivers. An assessment may reveal strengths, weaknesses, opportunities, or threats for some area of interest. The name of an assessment should be a noun or a short sentence.	Assessment
Goal	An end state that a stakeholder intends to achieve. Goals are generally expressed using qualitative words; for example, "increase", "improve", or "easier". Goals can also be decomposed; for example, "increase profit" can be decomposed into the goals "reduce cost" and "increase sales".	Goal

Concept	Definition	Notation
Requirement	A statement of need that must be realized by a system. Requirements represent the means to realize goals. The name of a requirement should be a short sentence.	Requirement
Constraint	A restriction on the way in which a system is realized. This may be a restriction on the implementation of the system (for example, specific technology that is to be used), or a restriction on the implementation process (for example, time or budget constraints). The name of a constraint should be a short sentence.	Constraint
Principle	A normative property of all systems in a given context, or the way in which they are realized. Principles are strongly related to goals and requirements. A principle defines a general property that applies to any system in a certain context. The name of a principle should be a short sentence.	Principle

7.2 Motivation Extension Relationships

The different types of relationships that can be used between two motivational elements and between one motivational element and one core element are show in Table 13.

Table 13: Motivation Extension Relationships

Intentional Relationships		Notation
Aggregation	Aggregation models that some intentional element is divided into multiple intentional elements.	◇————

Intentional Relationships		Notation
Realization	Realization models that some end is realized by some means. It is used to represent the following means-end relationships: A goal (the end) is realized by a principle, constraint, or requirement (the means). A principle (the end) is realized by a constraint or requirement (the means). A requirement (the end) is realized by a system (the means), which can be represented by an active structure element, a behavior element, or a passive structure element.	┈┈┈┈▷
Influence	Influence models that some motivational element has a positive or negative influence on the realization of another motivational element. A positive influence relationship does not imply that the realization of the influenced motivational element depends on the contributing intention. A negative influence relationship does not imply that the realization of the influenced motivational element is completely excluded by the contributing motivational element.	╌ ╌ ╌ ▶

As shown in Figure 15, a requirement or constraint can be related directly to a core element by means of a realization relationship. Other motivational elements cannot be related directly to core elements, but only indirectly by means of derived relationships via requirements or constraints.

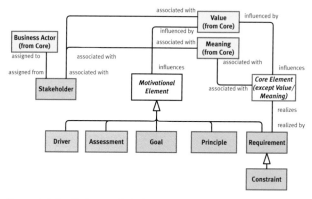

Figure 15: Relationships between Motivation Extension and the ArchiMate Core Concepts

7.3 Example

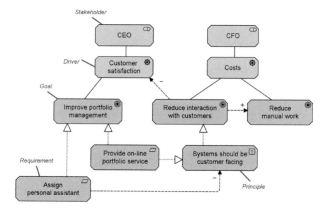

Figure 16: Example of a Motivation Extension Model

In this example, there are two key **stakeholders**, the "CEO" and the "CFO". The "CEO" has "Customer satisfaction" as a **driver**, with an associated goal of "Improve portfolio management". The CFO meanwhile has "Costs" as a driver, which has two associated **goals** of "Reduced interaction with customer" and "Reduce manual work". The "Reduce interaction with customers" goal is shown to have a positive influence on the "Reduce manual work" goal and is also likely to have a negative influence on the "Customer satisfaction" driver.

Two **requirements** "Assign personal assistant" and "Provide on-line portfolio service" are two alternative ways to realize the portfolio management **goal**. The second of these requirements also realizes the **principle** that "Systems should be customer facing" which, in turn, realizes the **goal** to "Reduce interaction with customers". The first **requirement** is shown to have a negative influence on the principle that "Systems should be customer-facing".

Chapter 8
The Implementation and Migration Extension

The Implementation and Migration Extension adds concepts to support the implementation and migration of architectures in Phase E (Opportunities and Solutions), Phase F (Migration Planning), and Phase G (Implementation Governance) of the TOGAF ADM.

This extension includes concepts for modeling implementation programs and projects to support program, portfolio, and project management, and a plateau concept to support migration planning.

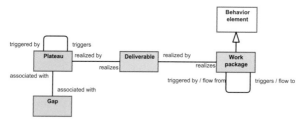

Figure 17: Implementation and Migration Extension Metamodel

8.1 Implementation and Migration Concepts

The central behavioral concept is a **work package**. A work package has a clearly defined beginning and end date, and a well-defined set of goals or results. The work package concept can be used at many levels to model projects, sub-projects, or tasks within a project, program, or project portfolio.

Work packages produce **deliverables**. These may be results of any kind, such as reports, papers, services, software, physical products, etc., or intangible results such as organizational change. A deliverable may also be the implementation of (a part of) an architecture.

The **plateau** concept is introduced to support the different states of an architecture in the TOGAF ADM, namely the Baseline, Target, and Transition Architecture states.

A **gap** is an outcome of the gap analysis technique of the TOGAF ADM, and forms an important input for the implementation and migration planning. The gap concept is linked to two plateaus (e.g., Baseline and Target Architecture, or two subsequent Transition Architectures), and represents the differences between these plateaus.

Table 14: Implementation and Migration Concepts

Concept	Definition	Notation
Work Package	A series of actions designed to accomplish a unique goal within a specified time.	Work package
Deliverable	A precisely-defined outcome of a work package.	Deliverable
Plateau	A relatively stable state of the architecture that exists during a limited period of time.	Plateau
Gap	An outcome of a gap analysis between two plateaus.	Gap

As shown in Figure 18, the implementation and migration concepts can be related to the ArchiMate Core concepts.

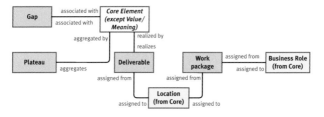

Figure 18: Relationships between Implementation and Migration Extension and the ArchiMate Core Concepts

8.2 Example

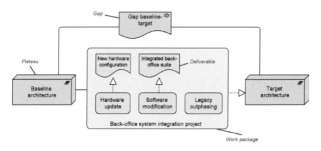

Figure 19: Example of an Implementation and Migration Extension Model

In this example, a "Baseline architecture" and "Target architecture" are defined and represented as **plateaus** – states which exist at a limited or particular point in time. The result of an analysis of the differences between the two plateaus is defined as a **gap**, referred to as "Gap baseline-target".

The "Back-office system integration project" **work package** is established and comprises of three lower-level **work packages**. "Hardware update" realizes a **deliverable** of providing a "New hardware configuration", "Software modification" realizes a **deliverable** of an "Integrated back-office suite", whilst the third lower-level work package "Legacy outphasing" has no identified deliverables. Undertaking the work packages results in the "Target architecture" plateau as an end state.

Chapter 9
ArchiMate Viewpoints

9.1 Viewpoint Classification

To help architects in selecting the right viewpoints for the task at hand, ArchiMate includes a framework for the definition and classification of viewpoints. The framework is based on two dimensions: **purpose** and **content**. The following three classifications support the **purpose** dimension:

- **Designing**: Design viewpoints support architects and designers in the design process from initial sketch to detailed design. Typically, design viewpoints consist of diagrams, like those used in, for example, UML.

- **Deciding**: Decision viewpoints assist managers in the process of decision-making by offering insight into cross-domain architecture relationships, typically through projections and intersections of underlying models, but also by means of analytical techniques. Typical examples are cross-reference tables, landscape maps, lists, and reports.

- **Informing**: Informing viewpoints help to inform any stakeholder about the enterprise architecture, in order to achieve understanding, obtain commitment, and convince adversaries. Typical examples are illustrations, animations, cartoons, flyers, etc.

For characterizing the **content** of a view ArchiMate defines the following abstraction levels:

- **Details**: Views on the detailed level typically consider one layer and one aspect from the ArchiMate framework. Typical stakeholders are a software engineer responsible for design and implementation of a software component or a process owner responsible for effective and efficient process execution. Examples of views are a BPMN process diagram and a UML class diagram.

- **Coherence**: At the coherence abstraction level, multiple layers or multiple aspects are spanned. Extending the view to more than one layer or aspect enables the stakeholder to focus on architecture relationships like process-uses-system (multiple layer) or application-uses-object (multiple aspect). Typical stakeholders are operational managers responsible for a collection of IT services or business processes.
- **Overview**: The overview abstraction level addresses both multiple layers and multiple aspects. Typically, such overviews are addressed to enterprise architects and decision-makers, such as CEOs and CIOs.

The dimensions of purpose and abstraction level are shown in Figure 20, together with examples of typical stakeholders that are addressed by these viewpoints. The top half of this figure shows the purpose dimension, while the bottom half shows the level of abstraction (or detail). Table 15 summarizes the different purposes and abstraction levels.

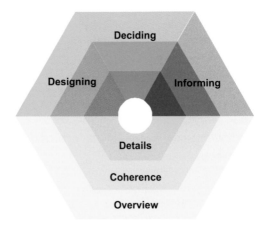

Figure 20: Viewpoint Purpose and Abstraction Levels

Table 15: Viewpoint Purpose and Abstraction Levels

	Typical Stakeholders	Purpose	Examples
Designing	architect, software developer, business process designer	navigate, design, support design decisions, compare alternatives	UML diagram, BPMN diagram, flowchart, ER diagram
Deciding	manager, CIO, CEO	decision-making	cross-reference table, landscape map, list, report
Informing	employee, customer, others	explain, convince, obtain commitment	animation, cartoon, process illustration, chart
Details	software engineer, process owner	design, manage	UML class diagram, BPMN process diagram
Coherence	operational managers	analyze dependencies, impact of-change	views expressing relationships like "use", "realize", and "assign"
Overview	enterprise architect, CIO, CEO	change management	landscape map

9.2 ArchiMate Viewpoints Summary

The following tables provide a summary of the viewpoints included in the ArchiMate 2.0 Standard.

Table 16: Standard Viewpoints

Viewpoint	Description
Introductory Viewpoint	This viewpoint uses a simplified notation to explain the essence of an architecture model to non-architects that require a simpler, more intuitive notation.
Organization Viewpoint	This viewpoint focuses on the (internal) organization of a company, a department, a network of companies, or of another organizational entity.

Viewpoint	Description
Actor Co-operation Viewpoint	This viewpoint focuses on the relationships of actors with each other and their environment.
Business Function Viewpoint	This viewpoint shows the main business functions of an organization and their relationships in terms of the flows of information, value, or goods between them.
Business Process Viewpoint	This viewpoint shows the high-level structure and composition of one or more business processes.
Business Process Co-operation Viewpoint	This viewpoint shows the relationships of one or more business processes with each other and/or with their environment.
Product Viewpoint	This viewpoint describes the value that one or more products offer to the customers or other external parties involved and shows the composition of one or more products in terms of the constituting (business or application) services, and the associated contract(s) or other agreements.
Application Behavior Viewpoint	This viewpoint describes the internal behavior of an application; e.g., as it realizes one or more application services.
Application Co-operation Viewpoint	This viewpoint describes the relationships between applications components in terms of the information flows between them, or in terms of the services they offer and use.
Application Structure Viewpoint	This viewpoint shows the structure of one or more applications or components.
Application Usage Viewpoint	This viewpoint describes how applications are used to support one or more business processes, and how they are used by other applications.
Infrastructure Viewpoint	This viewpoint describes the software and hardware infrastructure elements supporting the Application Layer, such as physical devices, networks, or system software (e.g., operating systems, databases, and middleware).
Infrastructure Usage Viewpoint	This viewpoint shows how applications are supported by the software and hardware infrastructure: the infrastructure services are delivered by the devices; system software and networks are provided to the applications.

Viewpoint	Description
Implementation and Deployment Viewpoint	This viewpoint shows how one or more applications are realized on the infrastructure.
Information Structure Viewpoint	This viewpoint shows the structure of the information used in the enterprise or in a specific business process or application, in terms of data types or (object-oriented) class structures.
Service Realization Viewpoint	This viewpoint shows how one or more business services are realized by the underlying processes (and sometimes by application components).
Layered Viewpoint	This viewpoint shows several layers and aspects of an enterprise architecture in a single diagram.
Landscape Map Viewpoint	This viewpoint uses a matrix to represent a three-dimensional co-ordinate system describing architectural relationships.

Table 17: Motivation Extension Viewpoints

Viewpoint	Description
Stakeholder Viewpoint	This viewpoint allows the analyst to model the stakeholders, the internal and external drivers for change, and the assessments (in terms of strengths, weaknesses, opportunities, and threats) of these drivers.
Goal Realization Viewpoint	This viewpoint allows a designer to model the refinement of (high-level) goals into more concrete goals, and the refinement of concrete goals into requirements or constraints that describe the properties that are needed to realize the goals.
Goal Contribution Viewpoint	This viewpoint allows a designer or analyst to model the influence relationships between goals and requirements.
Principles Viewpoint	This viewpoint allows the analyst or designer to model the principles that are relevant to the design problem at hand, including the goals that motivate these principles.
Requirements Realization Viewpoint	This viewpoint allows the designer to model the realization of requirements by the core elements, such as business actors, business services, business processes, application services, application components, etc.

Viewpoint	Description
Motivation Viewpoint	This viewpoint allows the designer or analyst to model the motivation aspect, without focusing on certain elements within this aspect.

Table 18: Implementation and Migration Extension Viewpoints

Viewpoint	Description
Project Viewpoint	This viewpoint is used to model the management of architecture change.
Migration Viewpoint	This viewpoint contains models and concepts that describe the transition from an existing architecture to a desired architecture.
Implementation and Migration Viewpoint	This viewpoint is used to relate programs and projects to the parts of the architecture that they implement.

9.3 Standard Viewpoints

9.3.1 Introductory Viewpoint

Summary	This viewpoint uses a simplified notation to explain the essence of an architecture model to non-architects that require a simpler, more intuitive notation.
Stakeholders	Enterprise architects, managers
Concerns	Make design choices visible, convince stakeholders
Purpose	Designing, deciding, informing
Abstraction Level	Coherence, Overview, Detail
Layer	Business, Application, and Technology Layers
Aspects	Structure, behavior, information

Concepts and Relationships

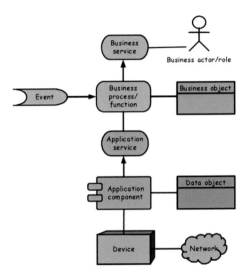

Example

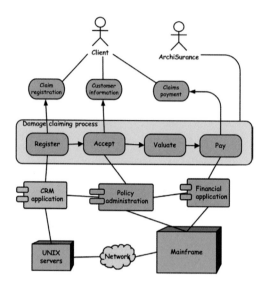

9.3.2 Organization Viewpoint

Summary	This viewpoint focuses on the (internal) organization of a company, a department, a network of companies, or of another organizational entity.
Stakeholders	Enterprise, process and domain architects, managers, employees, shareholders
Concerns	Identification of competencies, authority, and responsibilities
Purpose	Designing, deciding, informing
Abstraction Level	Coherence
Layer	Business Layer
Aspects	Structure

Concepts and Relationships

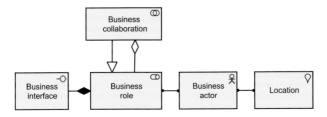

Example

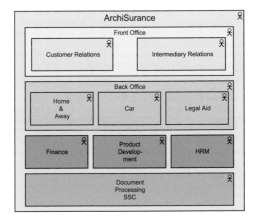

9.3.3 Actor Co-operation Viewpoint

Summary	This viewpoint focuses on the relationships of actors with each other and their environment.
Stakeholders	Enterprise, process, and domain architects
Concerns	Relationships of actors with their environment
Purpose	Designing, deciding, informing
Abstraction Level	Detail
Layer	Business Layer (Application Layer)
Aspects	Structure, behavior

Concepts and Relationships

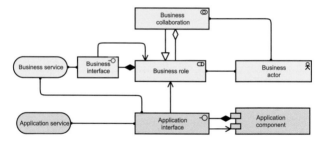

Example

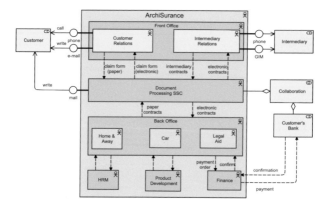

9.3.4 Business Function Viewpoint

Summary	This viewpoint shows the main business functions of an organization and their relationships in terms of the flows of information, value, or goods between them.
Stakeholders	Process and domain architects, operational managers
Concerns	Structure of business processes, consistency and completeness, responsibilities
Purpose	Designing
Abstraction Level	Detail
Layer	Business Layer
Aspects	Behavior

Concepts and Relationships

Example

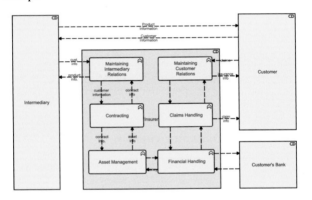

9.3.5 Business Process Viewpoint

Summary	This viewpoint shows the high-level structure and composition of one or more business processes.
Stakeholders	Process and domain architects, operational managers
Concerns	Structure of business processes, consistency and completeness, responsibilities
Purpose	Designing
Abstraction Level	Detail
Layer	Business Layer
Aspects	Behavior

Concepts and Relationships

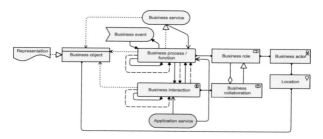

Example

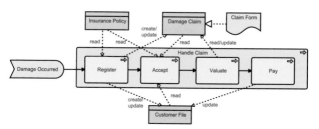

9.3.6 Business Process Co-operation Viewpoint

Summary	This viewpoint shows the relationships of one or more business processes with each other and/or with their environment.
Stakeholders	Process and domain architects, operational managers
Concerns	Dependencies between business processes, consistency and completeness, responsibilities
Purpose	Designing, deciding
Abstraction Level	Coherence
Layer	Business Layer, Application Layer
Aspects	Behavior

Concepts and Relationships

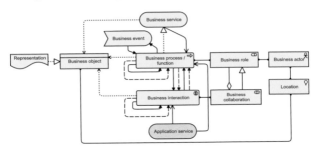

Example

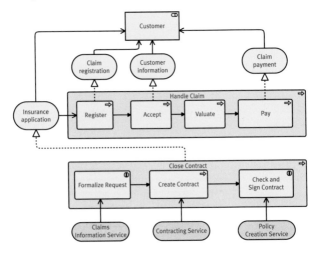

9.3.7 Product Viewpoint

Summary	This viewpoint describes the value that one or more products offer to the customers or other external parties involved and shows the composition of one or more products in terms of the constituting (business or application) services, and the associated contract(s) or other agreements.
Stakeholders	Product developers, product managers, process and domain architects
Concerns	Product development, value offered by the products of the enterprise
Purpose	Designing, deciding
Abstraction Level	Coherence
Layer	Business Layer, Application Layer
Aspects	Behavior, information

Concepts and Relationships

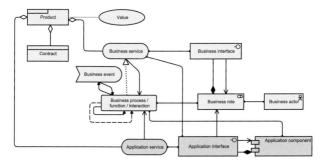

Example

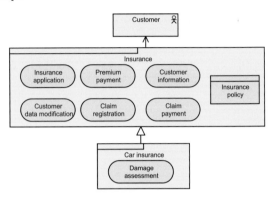

9.3.8 Application Behavior Viewpoint

Summary	This viewpoint describes the internal behavior of an application; e.g., as it realizes one or more application services.
Stakeholders	Enterprise, process, application, and domain architects
Concerns	Structure, relationships and dependencies between applications, consistency and completeness, reduction of complexity
Purpose	Designing
Abstraction Level	Coherence, details
Layer	Application Layer
Aspects	Information, behavior, structure

Concepts and Relationships

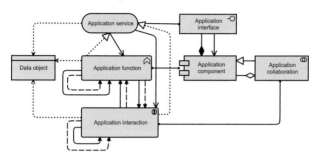

Example

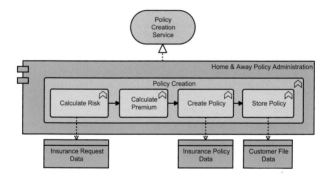

9.3.9 Application Co-operation Viewpoint

Summary	This viewpoint describes the relationships between applications components in terms of the information flows between them, or in terms of the services they offer and use.
Stakeholders	Enterprise, process, application, and domain architects
Concerns	Relationships and dependencies between applications, orchestration/choreography of services, consistency and completeness, reduction of complexity
Purpose	Designing
Abstraction Level	Coherence, details
Layer	Application Layer
Aspects	Behavior, structur

Concepts and Relationships

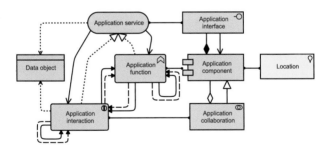

Example

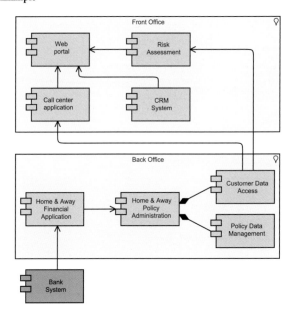

9.3.10 Application Structure Viewpoint

Summary	This viewpoint shows the structure of one or more applications or components.
Stakeholders	Enterprise, process, application, and domain architects
Concerns	Application structure, consistency and completeness, reduction of complexity
Purpose	Designing
Abstraction Level	Details
Layer	Application Layer
Aspects	Structure, information

Concepts and Relationships

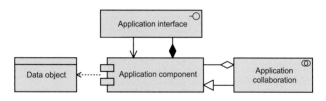

Example

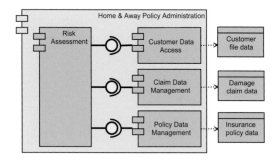

9.3.11 Application Usage Viewpoint

Summary	This viewpoint describes how applications are used to support one or more business processes, and how they are used by other applications.
Stakeholders	Enterprise, process, and application architects, operational managers
Concerns	Consistency and completeness, reduction of complexity
Purpose	Designing, deciding
Abstraction Level	Coherence
Layer	Business and Application Layers
Aspects	Behavior, structure

Concepts and Relationships

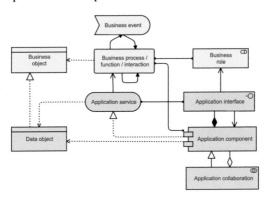

Example

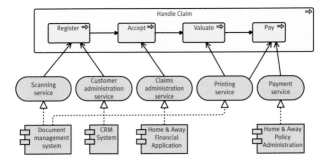

9.3.12 Infrastructure Viewpoint

Summary	This viewpoint describes the software and hardware infrastructure elements supporting the Application Layer, such as physical devices, networks, or system software (e.g., operating systems, databases, and middleware).
Stakeholders	Infrastructure architects, operational managers
Concerns	Stability, security, dependencies, costs of the infrastructure
Purpose	Designing
Abstraction Level	Details
Layer	Technology Layer
Aspects	Behavior, structure

Concepts and Relationships

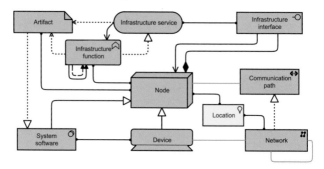

Example

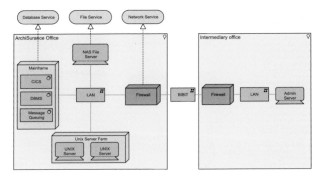

9.3.13 Infrastructure Usage Viewpoint

Summary	This viewpoint shows how applications are supported by the software and hardware infrastructure: the infrastructure services are delivered by the devices; system software and networks are provided to the applications.
Stakeholders	Application, infrastructure architects, operational managers
Concerns	Dependencies, performance, scalability
Purpose	Designing
Abstraction Level	Coherence
Layer	Application and Technology Layers
Aspects	Behavior, structure

Concepts and Relationships

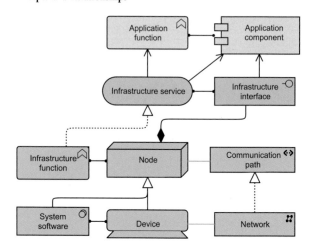

Example

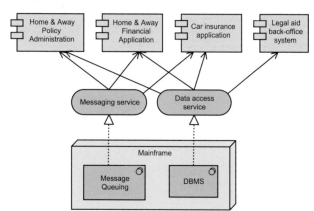

9.3.14 Implementation and Deployment Viewpoint

Summary	This viewpoint shows how one or more applications are realized on the infrastructure.
Stakeholders	Application and infrastructure architects, operational managers
Concerns	Dependencies, security, risks
Purpose	Designing
Abstraction Level	Coherence
Layer	Application Layer, Technology Layer
Aspects	Information, behavior, structure

Concepts and Relationships

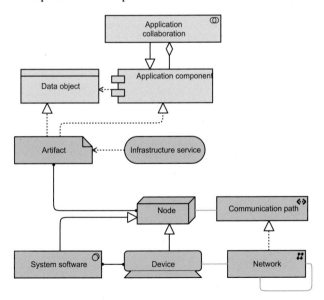

Example

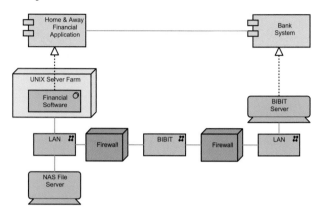

9.3.15 Information Structure Viewpoint

Summary	This viewpoint shows the structure of the information used in the enterprise or in a specific business process or application, in terms of data types or (object-oriented) class structures.
Stakeholders	Domain and information architects
Concerns	Structure and dependencies of the used data and information, consistency and completeness
Purpose	Designing
Abstraction Level	Details
Layer	Business Layer, Application Layer, Technology Layer
Aspects	Information

Concepts and Relationships

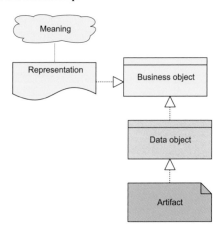

Example

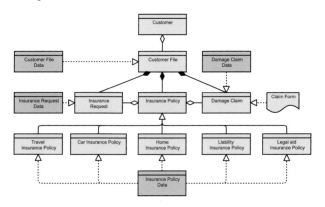

9.3.16 Service Realization Viewpoint

Summary	This viewpoint shows how one or more business services are realized by the underlying processes (and sometimes by application components).
Stakeholders	Process and domain architects, product and operational managers
Concerns	Added-value of business processes, consistency and completeness, responsibilities
Purpose	Designing, deciding
Abstraction Level	Coherence
Layer	Business Layer (Application Layer)
Aspects	Behavior, structure, information

Concepts and Relationships

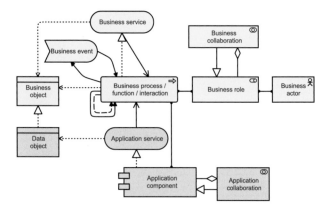

Example

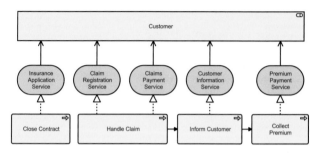

9.3.17 Layered Viewpoint

Summary	This viewpoint shows several layers and aspects of an enterprise architecture in a single diagram.
Stakeholders	Enterprise, process, application, infrastructure, and domain architects
Concerns	Consistency, reduction of complexity, impact of change, flexibility
Purpose	Designing, deciding, informing
Abstraction Level	Overview
Layer	Business Layer, Application Layer, Technology Layer
Aspects	Information, behavior, structure

Concepts and Relationships

All concepts and all relationships.

Example

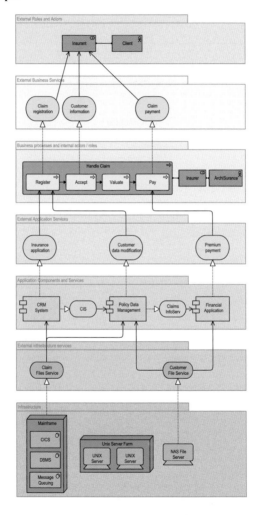

9.3.18 Landscape Map Viewpoint

Summary	This viewpoint uses a matrix to represent a three-dimensional co-ordinate system describing architectural relationships.
Stakeholders	Enterprise architects, top managers: CEO, CIO
Concerns	Readability, management and reduction of complexity, comparison of alternatives
Purpose	Deciding
Abstraction Level	Overview
Layer	Business Layer, Application Layer, Technology Layer
Aspects	Information, behavior, structure

Concepts and Relationships

All concepts and all relationships.

Example

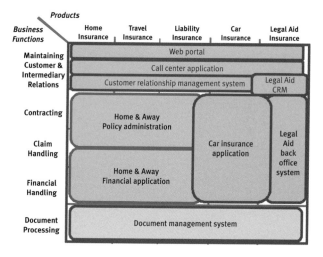

9.4 Motivation Extension Viewpoints

9.4.1 Stakeholder Viewpoint

Summary	This viewpoint allows the analyst to model the stakeholders, the internal and external drivers for change, and the assessments (in terms of strengths, weaknesses, opportunities, and threats) of these drivers.
Stakeholders	Stakeholders, business managers, enterprise and ICT architects, business analysts, requirements managers
Concerns	Architecture mission and strategy, motivation
Purpose	Designing, deciding, informing
Abstraction Level	Coherence, Details
Layer	Business, Application, and Technology Layers
Aspects	Motivation

Concepts and Relationships

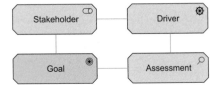

Example

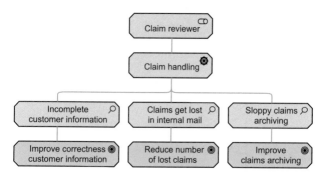

9.4.2 Goal Realization Viewpoint

Summary	This viewpoint allows a designer to model the refinement of (high-level) goals into more concrete goals, and the refinement of concrete goals into requirements or constraints that describe the properties that are needed to realize the goals.
Stakeholders	Stakeholders, business managers, enterprise and ICT architects, business analysts, requirements managers
Concerns	Architecture mission, strategy and tactics, motivation
Purpose	Designing, deciding
Abstraction Level	Coherence, Details
Layer	Business, Application, and Technology Layers
Aspects	Motivation

Concepts and Relationships

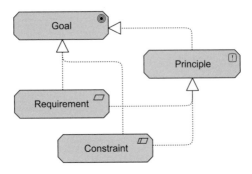

Example

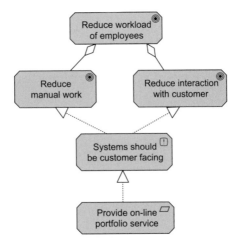

9.4.3 Goal Contribution Viewpoint

Summary	This viewpoint allows a designer or analyst to model the influence relationships between goals and requirements.
Stakeholders	Stakeholders, business managers, enterprise and ICT architects, business analysts, requirements managers
Concerns	Architecture mission, strategy and tactics, motivation
Purpose	Designing, deciding
Abstraction Level	Coherence, Details
Layer	Business, Application, and Technology Layers
Aspects	Motivation

Concepts and Relationships

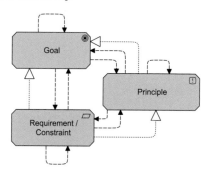

Example

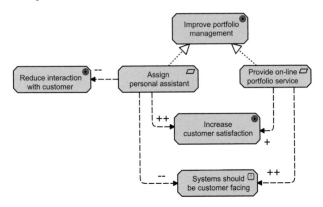

9.4.4 Principles Viewpoint

Summary	This viewpoint allows the analyst or designer to model the principles that are relevant to the design problem at hand, including the goals that motivate these principles.
Stakeholders	Stakeholders, business managers, enterprise and ICT architects, business analysts, requirements managers
Concerns	Architecture mission and strategy, motivation
Purpose	Designing, deciding, informing
Abstraction Level	Coherence, Details
Layer	Business, Application, and Technology Layers
Aspects	Motivation

Concepts and Relationships

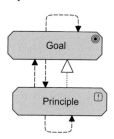

Example

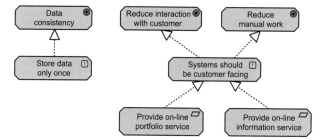

9.4.5 Requirements Realization Viewpoint

Summary	This viewpoint allows the designer to model the realization of requirements by the core elements, such as business actors, business services, business processes, application services, application components, etc.
Stakeholders	Enterprise and ICT architects, business analysts, requirements managers
Concerns	Architecture strategy and tactics, motivation
Purpose	Designing, deciding, informing
Abstraction Level	Coherence, Details
Layer	Business, Application, and Technology Layers
Aspects	Motivation

Concepts and Relationships

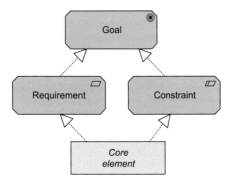

Example

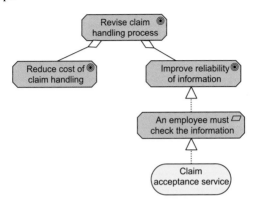

9.4.6 Motivation Viewpoint

Summary	This viewpoint allows the designer or analyst to model the motivation aspect, without focusing on certain elements within this aspect.
Stakeholders	Enterprise and ICT architects, business analysts, requirements managers
Concerns	Architecture strategy and tactics, motivation
Purpose	Designing, deciding, informing
Abstraction Level	Overview, Coherence, Details
Layer	Business, Application, and Technology Layers
Aspects	Motivation

Concepts and Relationships

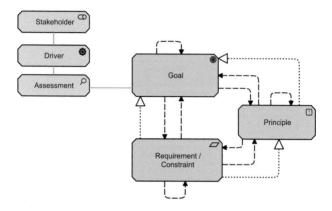

Example

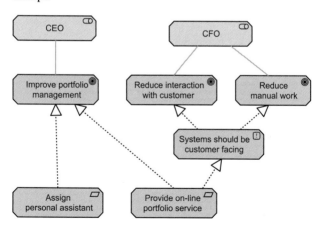

9.5 Implementation and Migration Viewpoints

9.5.1 Project Viewpoint

Summary	This viewpoint is used to model the management of architecture change.
Stakeholders	(operational) managers, enterprise and ICT architects, employees, shareholders
Concerns	Architecture vision and policies, motivation
Purpose	Deciding, informing
Abstraction Level	Overview
Layers/Extensions	Implementation and Migration Extension
Aspects	Information, behavior, structure

Concepts and Relationships

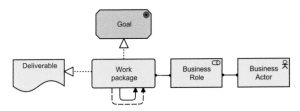

Example

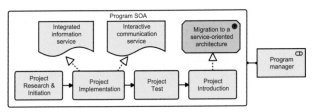

9.5.2 Migration Viewpoint

Summary	This viewpoint contains models and concepts that describe the transition from an existing architecture to a desired architecture.
Stakeholders	Enterprise architects, process architects, application architects, infrastructure architects and domain architects, employees, shareholders
Concerns	History of models
Purpose	Designing, deciding, informing
Abstraction Level	Overview
Layers/ Extensions	Implementation and Migration Extension
Aspects	Not applicable.

Concepts and Relationships

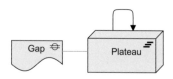

Example

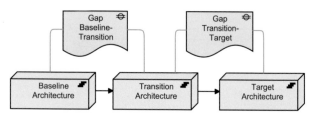

9.5.3 Implementation and Migration Viewpoint

Summary	This viewpoint is used to relate programs and projects to the parts of the architecture that they implement.
Stakeholders	(operational) managers, enterprise and ICT architects, employees, shareholders
Concerns	Architecture vision and policies, motivation
Purpose	Deciding, informing
Abstraction Level	Overview
Layers/ Extensions	Business Layer, Application Layer, Technology Layer, Implementation and Migration Extension
Aspects	Information, behavior, structure

Concepts and Relationships

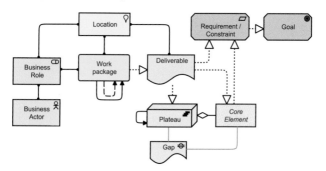

Example

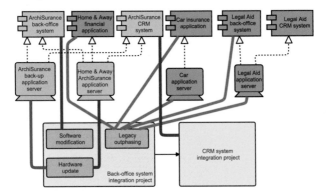

Chapter 10
ArchiSurance Case Study

The ArchiSurance Case Study is a fictitious example developed to illustrate the use of the ArchiMate modeling language in the context of the TOGAF framework. The Case Study concerns the insurance company ArchiSurance, which has been formed as the result of a merger of three previously independent companies. The Case Study describes the baseline architectures of the companies and then a change scenario.

ArchiSurance Case Study
This chapter is an abridged version of the ArchiSurance Case Study. The full case study can be obtained from The Open Group online bookstore at www.openroup.org/bookstore/catalog.

10.1 Background

ArchiSurance is the result of a recent merger of three previously independent insurance companies:

- Home & Away, specializing in homeowners' insurance and travel
- PRO-FIT, specializing in auto insurance
- Legally Yours, specializing in legal expense insurance

The company now consists of three divisions with the same names and headquarters as their predecessors.

ArchiSurance was formed to take advantage of numerous synergies between the three organizations. While the three pre-merger companies sold different types of insurance, they had similar business models. All three sold direct to consumers and small businesses through the web, email, telephone, and postal mail channels. Although based in different cities, each was completely housed in a modern office complex in a major metropolitan area. Each had loyal customer bases and strong reputations for integrity, value, service, and financial stability. All three companies were privately held by interlocking groups of institutional and individual investors.

Forces driving the merger were as follows:
- Lower-cost competitors were entering their markets
- New opportunities in high-growth regions
- Each company required significant new IT investments to remain competitive

Only a larger, combined company could simultaneously:
- Control costs
- Maintain customer satisfaction
- Invest in new technology
- Take advantage of emerging markets with high growth potential

The new company offers all the insurance products of the three pre-merger companies, and intends to frequently adjust its offerings in response to changing market conditions. Like its three predecessors, ArchiSurance sells directly to customers via print, web, and direct marketing.

To guide future changes in their business and information technology, ArchiSurance has decided to develop an enterprise architecture based on TOGAF 9.1 and ArchiMate 2.0 with minimal tailoring.

10.2 Preliminary Phase

In the Preliminary Phase, the main stakeholders in the architecture engagement and their concerns are identified. TOGAF defines a Stakeholder Map matrix as a technique to represent this. In ArchiMate, this can be expressed using the Stakeholder viewpoint, a fragment of which is shown as follows:

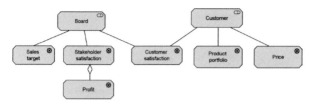

Figure 21: Fragment of a Stakeholder View

Figure 21 identifies two stakeholders (the ArchiSurance board of directors and its current and potential customers) and their concerns, modeled as drivers. Customer satisfaction is a shared concern of both stakeholders. Stakeholder satisfaction can be refined into more detailed concerns; e.g., profit.

Drivers motivate the development of specific business goals, as shown below for profit. Goals such as cost reduction can be partitioned into the reduction of maintenance costs and the reduction of personnel costs.

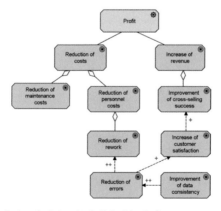

Figure 22: Business Goals Associated with the Driver Profit

The ArchiMate Principles viewpoint depicts principles, their dependencies, and the goals they realize in a graphical way:

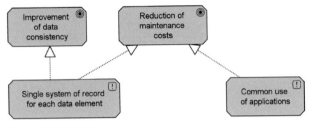

Figure 23: Principles View

10.3 Phase B: Baseline Business Architecture

After the merger, ArchiSurance set up a shared front-office as a multi-channel contact center for sales and customer service, with a primary contact center at the pre-merger headquarters of Home & Away. There are still three separate back-offices that handle the insurance products of the three original companies. A Shared Service Center (SSC) has been established for document processing at the pre-merger headquarters of PRO-FIT. The center administers the central document repository as well as all automated document workflows. In addition, it performs all scanning, printing, and archiving for legally binding documents as they enter or leave ArchiSurance. To ensure business continuity and handle periods of peak activity, the SSC also hosts trained personnel and equipment to perform the functions of the front-office, which is similarly prepared to reciprocate.

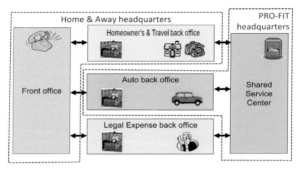

Figure 24: Global Organizational Structure of ArchiSurance

10.3.1 Organization Structure

The organization structure can be represented as a tree, as shown in Figure 25. This view shows the high-level organization structure of ArchiSurance, with its main locations and departments.

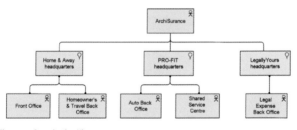

Figure 25: Organization View

10.3.2 Business Functions

The main business functions that ArchiSurance distinguishes are:

* Marketing, which studies, plans, promotes, and manages products and market segments, and works with Actuarial to design products

- Actuarial, which determines product prices and reserve levels, works with marketing to design new products, and analyzes enterprise risk
- Customer Relations, which includes the interactions between ArchiSurance and its customers; it handles customer questions, captures incoming claims, and conducts direct marketing campaigns
- Underwriting, which sets prices for individual policies and generates insurance proposals and policies
- Claims, which formulates and executes ArchiSurance's response to each claim against one of its policies
- Finance, which includes regular premium collection, according to the insurance policies with customers as produced by Contracting, and handles the payment of insurance claims
- Document Processing, which supports other functions through document scanning, printing, and archiving
- Investment Management, which manages financial and real estate assets for maximum returns within corporate and regulatory liquidity and risk constraints

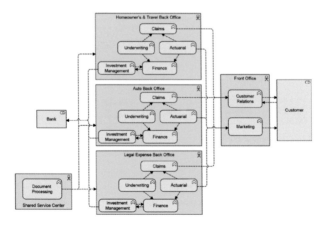

Figure 26: Business Function View

Some of these business functions are replicated in the three divisional back-offices of ArchiSurance.

Figure 26 shows the main business functions of ArchiSurance, as well as the most important information flows between the functions and external roles. It also shows the replication of business functions in the back-offices of the different divisions.

10.3.3 Business Processes

An ArchiMate business process groups behavior based on an ordering of activities. It produces a defined set of products or services. A process architecture shows the most important business processes and their relationships, and possibly the main steps within each of the processes. It usually does not show all the details of a process flow, which is the purpose of business process design languages.

Figure 27 shows the two central business processes of ArchiSurance, with their high-level sub-processes: Close contract, which is performed when selling a new insurance product, and Handle claim, which is performed when a damage claim has been received. While the details of these processes may differ for the different types of insurance product, the main steps are the same.

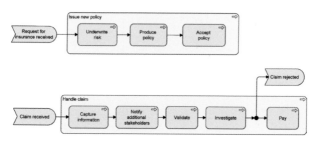

Figure 27: Business Process View

10.4 Phase C: Baseline Information Systems Architectures – Application Architecture

Since the merger, the three divisions have adopted a common web portal, contact center software suite, and document management system. Also, the company has selected a strategic CRM solution and implemented it for both Home & Away and PRO-FIT. However, due to management's focus on minimizing post-merger risks while continually improving the day-to-day performance of each division, core business application rationalization has not begun. Now that ArchiSurance has met post-merger performance expectations, investors expect substantial IT cost savings through the adoption of a common set of product and customer-focused applications. Therefore, a number of challenges remain. Home & Away still uses its pre-merger policy administration and financial application packages, while PRO-FIT and Legally Yours still use their own pre-merger custom monolithic applications.

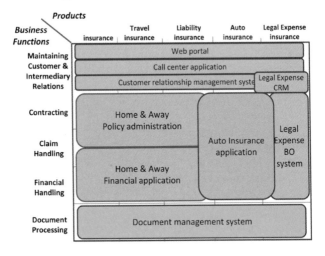

Figure 28: Application Landscape

10.4.1 Application Co-operation

ArchiMate defines an Application Co-operation viewpoint to show an overview of the application landscape and the dependencies between the applications.

The TOGAF counterpart of this viewpoint is the Application Communication diagram. Figure 29 shows the main applications of ArchiSurance, as well as the main data flows between the applications.

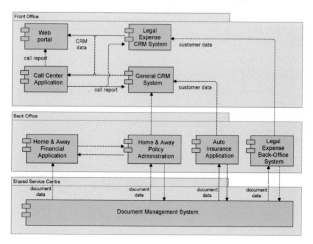

Figure 29: Application Co-Operation View

10.4.2 Business-Application Alignment

TOGAF specifies matrix-based viewpoints to show the links between the business and the application architecture; e.g. an Application/Organization matrix and an Application/Function matrix.

The relationships between application components can also be modeled graphically. ArchiMate defines the Application Usage viewpoint:

The Application Usage viewpoint describes how applications are used to support one or more business processes, and how they are used by other applications. It can be used in designing an application by identifying the services needed by business processes and other applications, or in designing business processes by describing the services that are available. Furthermore, since it identifies the dependencies of business processes upon applications, it may be useful to operational managers responsible for these processes.

The Application Service concept plays a central role in this viewpoint. Figure 30 shows a subset of the services offered by the applications used by the Home & Away division of ArchiSurance, and which of the sub-processes of the claim handling process make use of which of these services.

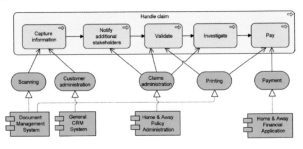

Figure 30: Application Usage View

10.5 Phase C: Baseline Information Systems Architectures – Data Architecture

Figure 31 shows a subset of the business objects that ArchiSurance defines. Part of the customer information is an insurance file, which is composed of insurance requests, insurance policies, and damage claims. A number of specializations of the insurance policy object are defined, one for each type of insurance that ArchiSurance sells.

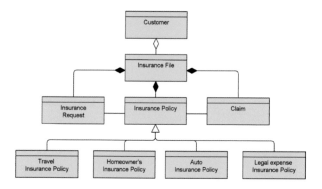

Figure 31: Information Structure View

Figure 32 shows a Data Dissemination diagram for one ArchiSurance application.

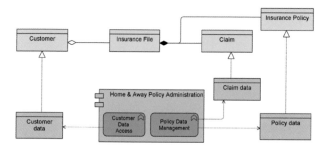

Figure 32: Data Dissemination Diagram

10.6 Phase D: Baseline Technology Architecture

Figure 33 sketches the technical infrastructure landscape of ArchiSurance. In the front-office, located at the Home & Away headquarters, there is a general-purpose server and one dedicated to web hosting. The Shared Service Center (SSC), located at the PRO-FIT headquarters, has its own server for the document management system. Each of the three back-offices has a server for its applications.

A Local Area Aetwork (LAN) connects servers and personal computers at each of the three ArchiSurance locations, which are in turn connected by a corporate Wide Area Network (WAN).

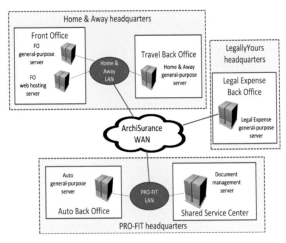

Figure 33: Infrastructure Landscape

Figure 34 shows the main infrastructure components of ArchiSurance, grouped by location and department. Also the networks that connect the different devices, and the (application) artifacts deployed on the devices, are shown in this view.

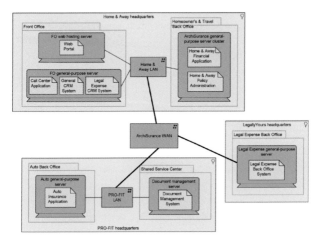

Figure 34: Infrastructure View

10.7 Change Scenario: Application Portfolio Rationalization

The inflexibility of the ArchiSurance application architecture makes it difficult to adapt to changes in business conditions. Partly as a result of the merger, the application landscape has become scattered, resulting in data redundancy and functional overlap, as well as point-to-point application integration using a variety of data formats and methods. These problems cause internal instabilities, increased application maintenance costs, and obstacles to sharing information across the company and with partners. Consequently, the IT department has a sizable backlog of work requests. ArchiSurance top management is very concerned about the backlog, particularly an unmet need to share information automatically with high-volume contracted sales partners and influential insurance consultants.

This scenario rationalizes the ArchiSurance application portfolio by:

- Migrating to an integrated back-office suite for functions such as policy administration and financial transactions. The suite will consist of:
  - *AUTO-U*, an automated underwriting system that generates proposals and policies
  - *P-ADMIN*, a packaged policy administration system that integrates with the automated underwriting system to issue, modify, and renew policies; this system also handles customer accounting and billing
  - *VERSA-CLAIM*, a packaged claims system with screens and workflow that can be configured to support ArchiSurance's three lines of business
  - *P-CONFIG*, a product configurator management used to define all insurance products, and expose these definitions to AUTO-U, P-ADMIN, and VERSA-CLAIM through web services
  - *BRIMS,* a business rule management system (BRMS) consisting of a rules repository, a processing engine, a rule development environment, and an authoring tool for rule management user interfaces. The business rule engine exposes rule execution capabilities to AUTO-U, P-ADMIN, VERSA-CLAIM, and P-CONFIG through web services.
- Completing the migration to the strategic CRM system

The ArchiSurance lead investors and CEO support these initiatives on the condition that all changes are invisible to ArchiSurance customers and partners. The insurer's products and services must not be affected, and all customer and partner interactions must proceed uninterrupted and unchanged.

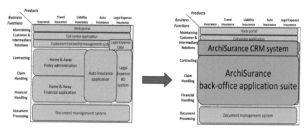

Figure 35: Application Portfolio Rationalization

As part of this effort, the technical infrastructure will also be simplified. The separate back-office servers will be replaced by a shared server cluster located in the data center at Home & Away headquarters. However, to ensure business continuity, there will also be a back-up server cluster located in the data center at PRO-FIT headquarters.

10.7.1 Phase A: Architecture Vision

Phase A of the TOGAF ADM establishes an architecture effort and initiates an iteration of the architecture development cycle by setting its scope, constraints, and goals. This phase also validates the business context and develops a Statement of Architecture Work.

The business context consists of the key business requirements based upon the main business goals and architecture principles. Some relevant business goals and principles for the current scenario are shown in Figure 36.

Goals and principles are the basis for concrete requirements, as shown in an ArchiMate Goal Refinement viewpoint in Figure 37.

An important element of the architecture vision is a high-level representation of the baseline and target architectures, to explain the

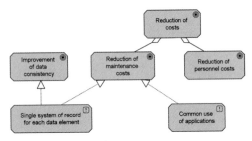

Figure 36: Business Goals and Principles

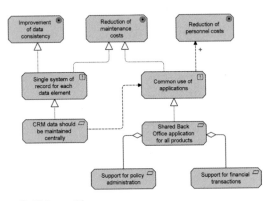

Figure 37: Goal Refinement View

added value of the architecture effort to stakeholders. The example below highlights the most important changes that are needed in the current change scenario using the Introductory Viewpoint:

- In the Front-Office, the separate CRM system for Legal Expense will disappear.
- In the Back-Office, the separate back-office applications will be replaced with a single back-office suite. The three separate general-purpose back-

office servers will be replaced by a shared server cluster and a back-up server cluster.

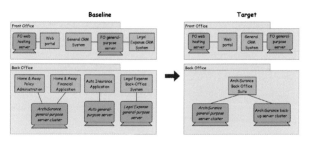

Figure 38: Introductory View

10.7.2 Phase B: Target Business Architecture and Gap Analysis

In this scenario, the business architecture remains unchanged. However, in the business architecture, we also show how the target architecture realizes the key business requirements. This can be expressed using the Requirements Realization viewpoint. The example below shows how the

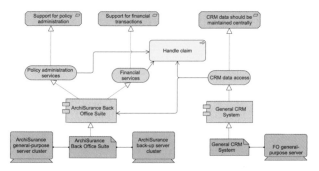

Figure 39: Requirements Realization View

business requirements established in the architecture vision phase are realized by elements in the architecture.

10.7.3 Phase C: Target Application Architecture and Gap Analysis

The Application Communication diagram below shows the proposed target situation for the application landscape.

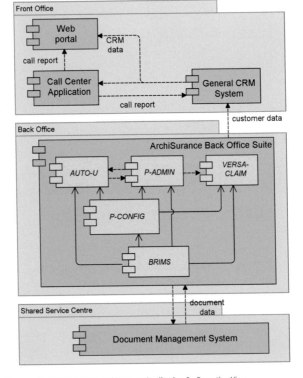

Figure 40: Target Application Architecture: Application Co-Operation View

The results of a global gap analysis for the application architecture are
visualized below. Several application components that exist in the baseline
architecture are no longer present in the target architecture: the separate
back-office applications and the separate Legal Expense insurance CRM
system. The CRM functionality for Legal Expense insurance customers
is taken over by the general CRM system; therefore, this does not require
new components (although it may be necessary to adapt or reconfigure
the existing general CRM system, this is not shown in the gap analysis). In
addition, a completely new back-office application suite is introduced.

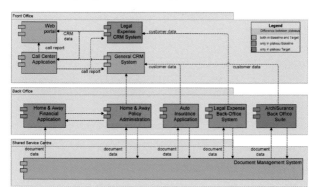

Figure 41: Application Architecture: Gap Analysis

10.7.4 Phase D: Target Technology Architecture and Gap Analysis

The Infrastructure view below shows the proposed target situation for the
technical infrastructure landscape.

Figure 43 visualizes the results of a global gap analysis for the technology
architecture. The separate general-purpose back-office servers are slated
for removal. The original server cluster of Home & Away is to become

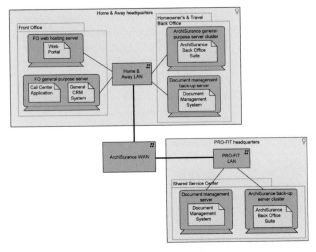

Figure 42: Target Technology Architecture: Infrastructure View

the central ArchiSurance back-office service cluster, and an additional back-up server cluster is to be placed in the SSC at PRO-FIT headquarters. There is also a back-up document management server to be placed in the Home & Away back-office. The new back-office suite and the document management system are to be replicated on their respective main servers and back-up servers.

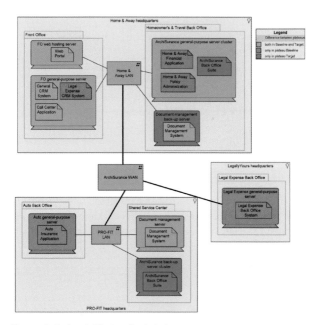

Figure 43: Technology Architecture: Gap Analysis

10.7.5 Implementation and Migration Planning

In ArchiMate, the baseline, target, and transition architectures, as well as their relationships, are shown using the Migration viewpoint. Figure 44 shows an example for the current scenario. The IT department of ArchiSurance does not have sufficient resources to carry out the integration of the back-office systems and the integration of the CRM systems in parallel. One transition architecture therefore replaces two CRM systems with one, but has separate back-office systems. Another has a single back-office suite but two CRM applications.

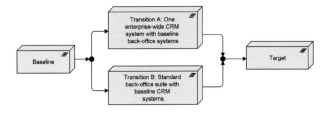

Figure 44: Migration View

Transition architectures enable the planning of implementation projects
such as CRM integration and back-office application integration. The
sequence of these projects depends on which of the transition architectures
is selected. This can be described using a TOGAF Project Context diagram,
as shown in Figure 45.

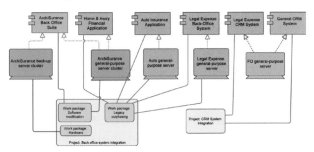

Figure 45: TOGAF Project Context Diagram, expressed in ArchiMate

Index